ON THE
ART
OF
TEACHING

HORACE MANN
1796-1859

ON THE
ART
OF
TEACHING

Horace Mann

Applewood Books

ISBN 978-1-55709-129-1

Printed in USA

20 19 18 17 16 15 14 13 12 11

On The Art Of Teaching

Horace Mann is, perhaps, the greatest name in the history of American education. In 1837, after a career in law and politics, he began what was to be a twelve-year term presiding over the Massachusetts Board of Education, the first in the country. In 1840, as part of his Fourth Annual Report of the Board of Education, Mann wrote *On the Art of Teaching*. Its message on the qualifications essential for those undertaking the momentous task of training children has lived on, as a timeless and inspiring appeal to some of our country's most dedicated servants.

KNOWLEDGE OF STUDIES

Teachers should have a perfect knowledge of the rudimental branches which are required by law to be taught in our schools. They should understand, not only the rules which have been prepared as guides for the unlearned but also the principles on which the rules are founded—those principles which lie beneath the rules and supersede them in practice, and from which, should the rules be lost, they could be framed anew. Teachers should be able to teach subjects, not manuals merely.

This knowledge should not only be thorough and critical but it should be always ready at command for every exigency; familiar

Teachers should have a thorough and critical knowledge of the subjects to be taught in our schools

A teacher's knowledge should be as familiar as the alphabet, so that it will rise up in the mind instantaneously

like the alphabet, so that, as occasion requires, it will rise up in the mind instantaneously and not need to be studied out with labor and delay. For instance; it is not enough that the teacher be able to solve and elucidate an arithmetical question by expending half an hour of schooltime in trying various ways to bring out the answer; for that half hour is an important part of the school session, and the regular exercises of the school must be shortened or slurred over to repair the loss.

Again; in no school can a teacher devote his whole and undivided attention to the exercises as they successively recur. Numerous things will demand simultaneous attention. While a class is spelling or reading, he may have occasion to recall the roving attention of one scholar; to admonish another by word or look; to answer some question put by a third; or to require a fourth to execute some needed service. Now, if he is not so familiar with the true orthography of every word that his ear will instantaneously detect an error in the spelling, he will, on all such occasions, pass by mistakes without notice, and therefore without correction, and thus interweave wrong instruction with right through all the lessons of the school. If he is not so familiar, too, both with the rules of reading, and with the standard of pronunciation for each word, that a wrong emphasis or cadence, or a mispronounced word, will jar his nerves and recall even a wandering attention, then innumerable errors will glide by his own ear unnoticed, while they are stamped upon the minds of his pupils.

These remarks apply with equal force to recitations in grammar and geography. A critical knowledge respecting all these subjects should be so consciously present with him that his mind will gratefully respond to every right answer or sign made by the scholar, and shrink from every wrong one, with the quickness and certainty of electrical attraction and repulsion....

There is no equivalent for a mastership in the rudiments

However much other knowledge a teacher may possess, it is no equivalent for a mastership in the rudiments. It is not more true in architecture than in education that the value of the work in every upper layer depends upon the solidity of all beneath it. The leading, prevailing defect in the intellectual department of our schools is a want of thoroughness, a proneness to be satisfied with a verbal memory of rules instead of a comprehension of principles, with a knowledge of the names of things, instead of a knowledge of the things themselves; or, if some knowledge of the things is gained, it is too apt to be a knowledge of them as isolated facts and unaccompanied by a knowledge of the relations which subsist between them and bind them into a scientific whole. That knowledge is hardly worthy of the name which stops with things, as individuals, without understanding the relations existing between them. The latter constitutes indefinitely the greater part of all human knowledge.

A child's limbs are as well fitted in point of strength to play with the planets before he can toss a ball as his mind is to get any conception of the laws which govern their stupendous motions before he is master of common arithmetic. For these and similar considerations, it seems that the first intellectual qualification of a teacher is a critical thoroughness, both in rules and principles, in regard to all the branches required by law to be taught in the common schools; and a power of recalling them in any of their parts with a promptitude and a certainty hardly inferior to that which he could tell his own name.

The first intellectual qualification of a teacher is a critical thoroughness, both in rules and principles

Aptness to Teach

The ability to acquire and the ability to impart are wholly different talents. The former may exist in the most liberal manner without the latter. It was a remark of Lord Bacon that "the art of well-delivering the knowledge we possess is among the secrets left to be discovered by future generations." Dr. Watts says, "There are some very learned men who know much themselves, but who have not the talent of communicating their knowledge." Indeed this fact is not now questioned by any intelligent educationist. Hence we account for the frequent complaints that those teachers who had sustained an examination in an acceptable manner failed in the schoolroom through a want of facility in communicating what they knew.

The ability to acquire and the ability to impart are wholly different talents

The ability to acquire is the power of understanding the subject matter of investigation. Aptness to teach involves the power of perceiving how far a scholar understands the subject matter to be learned, and what, in the natural order, is the next step he is to take. It involves the power of discovering and of solving at the time the exact difficulty by which the learner is embarrassed. The removal of a slight impediment, the drawing aside of the thinnest veil which happens to divert his steps or obscure his vision is worth more to him than volumes of lore on collateral subjects.

How much does the pupil comprehend of the subject? What should his next step be? Is his mind looking toward a truth or an error? The answer to these questions must be intuitive in the person who is apt to teach. As a dramatic writer throws himself successively into the characters of the drama he is com-

Aptness to teach is the power to perceive how well a student understands the subject and to know the next step

posing that he may express the ideas and emotions peculiar to each, so the mind of a teacher should migrate, as it were, into those of his pupils to discover what they know and feel and need; and then, supplying from his own stock what they require, he should reduce it to such a form and bring it within such a distance that they can reach out and seize and appropriate it.

The mind of a teacher should migrate into the minds of the pupils to discover what they know and feel and need

He should never forget that intellectual truths are naturally adapted to give intellectual pleasure; and that, by leading the minds of his pupils onward to such a position in relation to these truths that they themselves can discover them, he secures to them the natural reward of a new pleasure with every new discovery, which is one of the strongest as well as most appropriate incitements to future exertion.

Intellectual truths naturally give pleasure

By leading pupils to discover these truths for themselves, the teacher gives them a natural reward with every new discovery

Aptness to teach includes the presentation of the different parts of a subject in a natural order. If a child is told that the globe is about 25,000 miles in circumference before he has any conception of the length of a mile, the statement is not only utterly useless as an act of instruction but it will probably prevent him ever afterward from gaining an adequate idea of the subject. The novelty will be gone, and yet the fact unknown. Besides, a systematic acquisition of a subject knits all parts of it together, so that they will be longer retained and more easily recalled. To acquire a few of the facts gives us fragments only; and even to master all the facts, but to obtain them promiscuously, leaves what is acquired so unconnected and loose that any part of it may be jostled out of its place and lost, or remain only to mislead.

A systematic acquisition of a subject knits all parts of it together

Aptness to teach, in fine, embraces a knowledge of methods and processes. These are indefinitely various. Some are adapted to accomplish their object in an easy and natural manner; others, in a toilsome and circuitous one; others, again, may accomplish the object at which they aim with certainty and dispatch, but secure it by inflicting deep and lasting injuries upon the social and moral sentiments. We are struck with surprise on learning, that, but a few centuries since, the feudal barons of Scotland, in running out the lines around their extensive domains, used to take a party of boys and whip them at the different posts and landmarks in order to give them a retentive memory as witnesses in case of future litigation or dispute. Though this might give them a vivid recollection of localities, yet it would hardly improve their ideas of justice or propitiate them to bear true testimony in favor of the chastiser. But do not those who have no aptness to teach sometimes accomplish their objects by a kindred method?

He who is apt to teach is acquainted, not only with common methods for common minds but with peculiar methods for pupils of peculiar dispositions and temperaments; and he is acquainted with the principles of all methods where by he can vary his plan according to any difference of circumstances.

Those who are apt to teach are acquainted with both common methods and unusual methods and know as many modes as cases that may arise

... [He should have] a knowledge of modes as various as the diversity of cases that may arise, that, like a skillful pilot, they may not only see the haven for which they are to steer but know every bend in the channel that leads to it . No one is so poor in resources for difficult emergencies as they may arise as he whose knowledge of methods is limited to the one in which he happened to be instructed. It is this way that rude nations go on for indefinite periods, imitating what they have seen and teaching only as they were taught.

The Art of Managing a Classroom

Experience has also proved that there is no necessary connection between literary competency, aptness to teach, and the power to manage and govern a school successfully. They are independent qualifications; yet a marked deficiency in any one of the three renders the other nearly valueless. In regard to the ordinary management or administration of a school, how much judgement is demanded in the organization of classes so that no scholar shall either be clogged and retarded, or hurried forward with injudicious speed, by being matched with an unequal yoke-fellow! Great discretion is necessary in the assignment of lessons in order to avoid, on the one hand, such shortness in the tasks as allows time

Judgement is demanded in the organization of classes so that no student shall either be slowed or hurried by being matched with an unequal partner

to be idle; and, on the other, such overassignments as render thoroughness and accuracy impracticable, and thereby so habituate the pupil to mistakes and imperfections that he cares little or nothing about committing them.

Lessons should be adjusted to the capacity of the scholar

Lessons, as far as it is possible, should be so adjusted to the capacity of the scholar that there should be no failure in a recitation not occasioned by culpable neglect. The sense of shame, or of regret for ignorance, can never be made exquisitely keen if the lessons given are so long or so difficult as to make failures frequent. When "bad marks," as they are called, against a scholar become common, they not only lose their salutary force but every addition to them debases his character, and carries him through a regular course of training which prepares him to follow in the footsteps of those convicts who are so often condemned, that, at length, they are nothing for the ignominy of the sentence. Yet all this may be the legitimate consequence of being unequally mated or injudiciously tasked. It is a sad sight, in any school to see a pupil marked for a deficiency without any blush of shame or sign of guilt; and it is never done with impunity to his moral character.

The preservation of order, together with the proper dispatch of business, requires a mean between the too much and the too little in all the evolutions of the school, which it is difficult to hit. When classes leave their seats for the recitation stand and return to them again, or when the different sexes have a recess, or the hour of intermission arrives, if there be not some order and succession of movement, the school will be temporarily converted into a promiscuous rabble, giving both the temptation and the opportunity for committing every species of in-

The preservation of order in the classroom requires a balance between the too much and the too little

decorum and aggression. In order to prevent confusion, on the other hand, the operations of the school may be conducted with such military formality and procrastination—the second scholar not being allowed to leave his seat until the first has reached the door or the place of recitation, and each being made to walk on tiptoe to secure silence—That a substantial part of every school session will be wasted in the wearisome pursuit of an object worth nothing when obtained.

When we reflect how many things are to be done each half day, and how short a time is allotted for their performance, the necessity of system in regard to all the operations of the school will be apparent. System compacts labor; and when the hand is to be turned to an almost endless variety of particulars, if system does not preside over the whole series of movements, the time allotted to each will be spent in getting

The operations of the school should be systemized so that everything that needs to be done can be done

ready to perform it. With lessons to set; with so many classes to hear; with difficulties to explain; with the studies to be assisted; the idle to be spurred; the transgressors to be admonished or corrected; with the goers and comers to observe; with all these things to be done, no considerable progress can be made if one part of the wheel is not coming up to the work while another is going down.

And if order do not pervade, in the school as a whole, and in all its parts, all is lost. And this is a very difficult thing; for it seems as though the school were only a point, rescued out of a chaos that still encompasses it, and is ready on the first opportunity to break in and reoccupy its ancient possession....

All is lost, unless order pervades the school

The government and discipline of a school demands qualities still more rare, because the consequences of error in these are still more disastrous. What caution,

Caution, wisdom, uprightness, and sometimes even intrepidity are necessary in the administration of punishment

wisdom, uprightness, and sometimes even intrepidity are necessary in the administration of punishment! After all other means have been tried, and tried in vain, the chastisement of pupils found to be otherwise incorrigible is still upheld by law and sanctioned by public opinion. But it is the last resort, the ultimate resource, acknowledged on all hands to be a relic of barbarism, and yet authorized because the community, although they feel it to be a great evil, have not yet devised and applied an antidote.

Through an ignorance of the laws of health, a parent may so corrupt the constitution of his child as to render poison a necessary medicine; and, through an ignorance of the laws of mind, he may do the same thing in regard to punishment. When the arts of health and of education are understood, neither poison nor punishment will need to be used, unless in most extraordinary cases. The discipline of former times was inexorably stern and severe; and, even if it were wished, it is impossible now to return to it. The question is, what can be substituted, which, without its severity, shall have its efficiency?....

A school should be governed with a steady hand, not only during the same season but from year to year; substantially the same extent of indulgence being allowed and the same restrictions imposed. It is injurious to the children to alternate between the extremes of an easy and a sharp discipline. It is unjust also for one teacher to profit by letting down the discipline of a school, and thus throw upon his successor the labor of raising it up to its former level.

A school should be governed with a steady hand

It is harmful to the children to alternate between extremes of discipline

Molding Good Behavior

The effects of civility or discourtesy, of gentlemanly or ungentlemanly deportment, are not periodical or occasional, merely, but of constant recurrence; and all the members of society have a direct interest in the manners of each of its individuals, because each one is a radiating point, the center of a circle which he fills with pleasure or annoyance, not only for those who voluntarily enter it but for those, who, in the promiscuous movements of society, are caught within its circumference. Good behavior includes the elements of that equity, benevolence, conscience, which, in their great combinations, the moralist treats of in his books of ethics and the legislator enjoins in his codes of law.

The schoolroom and its play-

The effects of good behaviour recur constantly

In the schoolroom, selfishness collides with social duty

ground, next to the family table, are the places where the selfish propensities come into most direct collision with social duties. Here, then, a right direction should be given to the growing mind. The surrounding influences which are incorporated into its new thoughts and feelings, and make part of their substance, are too minute and subtle to be received in masses like nourishment; they are rather imbibed into the system unconsciously by every act of respiration, and are constantly insinuating themselves into it through all the avenues of the senses. If, then, the manners of the teacher are to be imitated by his pupils, if he is the glass at which they "do dress themselves," how strong is the necessity that he should understand those nameless and innumerable practices in regard to deportment, dress, conversation, and all personal habits that constitute the difference between a gentleman and a clown!

We can fear some oddity or eccentricity in a friend whom we admire for his talents or revere for his virtues; but it becomes quite a different thing when the oddity or the eccentricity is to be a pattern or model from which fifty or a hundred children are to form their manners. It is well remarked by the ablest British traveler who has ever visited this country that, among us, "every male above twenty-one years of age claims to be a sovereign. He is, therefore, *bound to be a gentleman.*"